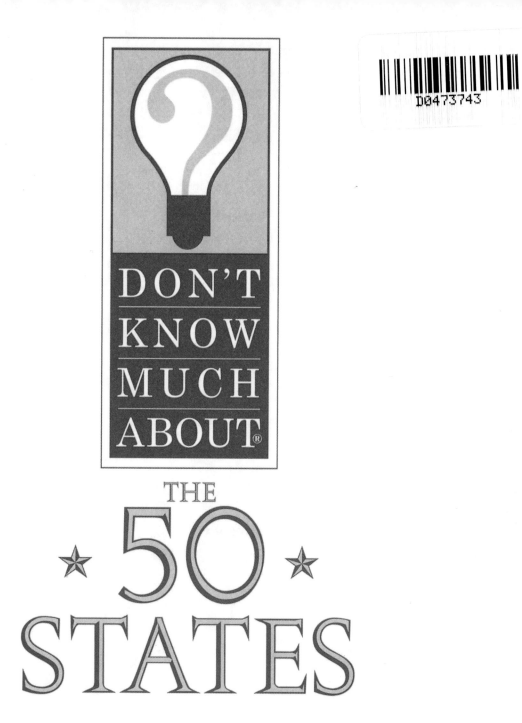

DON'T
KNOW
MUCH
ABOUT®

THE
★ 50 ★
STATES

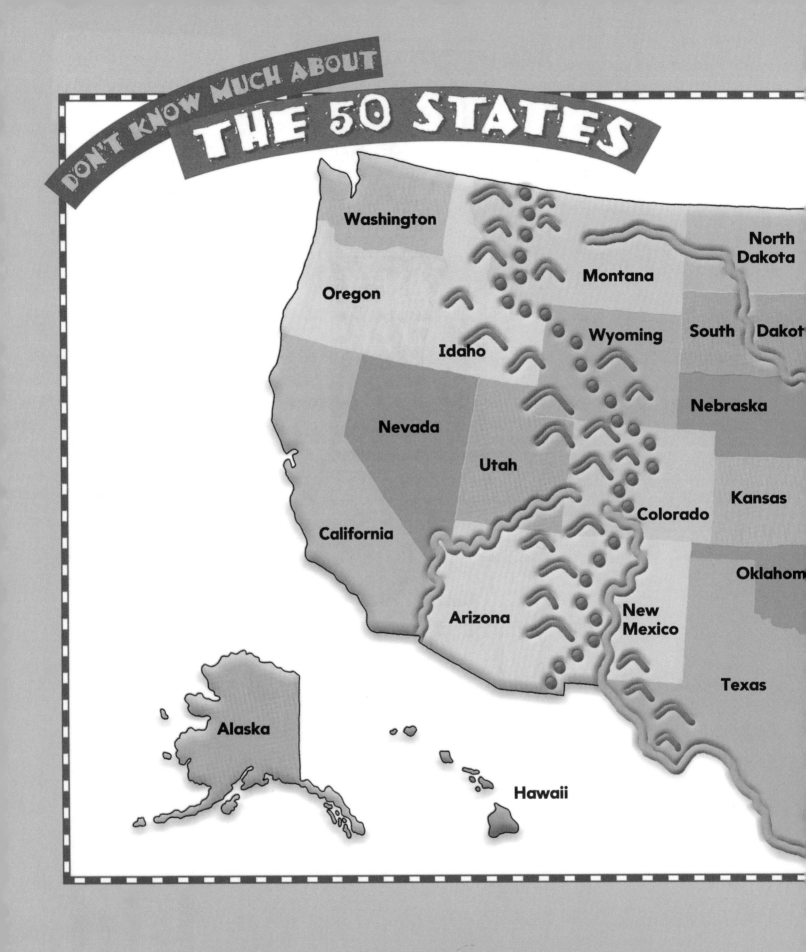

DON'T KNOW MUCH ABOUT **THE 50 STATES**

Washington

Oregon

Idaho

Nevada

Utah

California

Arizona

Montana

Wyoming

North Dakota

South Dakot

Nebraska

Colorado

Kansas

New Mexico

Oklahom

Texas

Alaska

Hawaii

THE UNITED STATES

Minnesota

Wisconsin

Michigan

Iowa

Ohio

Indiana

Illinois

Missouri

Kentucky

Arkansas

Tennessee

Vermont

Maine

New Hampshire

Massachusetts

New York

Rhode Island

Connecticut

Pennsylvania

New Jersey

West Virginia

Delaware

Maryland

Virginia

North Carolina

South Carolina

Alabama

Georgia

Florida

Mississippi

Louisiana

The Thirteen Original Colonies

Connecticut

Delaware

Georgia

Maryland

Massachusetts

New Hampshire

New Jersey

New York

North Carolina

Pennsylvania

Rhode Island

South Carolina

Virginia

DON'T KNOW MUCH ABOUT®

THE
★ 50 ★
STATES

KENNETH C. DAVIS
ILLUSTRATED BY RENÉE ANDRIANI

SCHOLASTIC INC.

New York Toronto London Auckland Sydney
Mexico City New Delhi Hong Kong Buenos Aires

Acknowledgments

An author's name goes on the cover of a book. But behind that book are a great many people who make it all happen. I would like to thank all of the wonderful people at HarperCollins who helped make this book a reality, including Susan Katz, Kate Morgan Jackson, Barbara Lalicki, Harriett Barton, Rosemary Brosnan, Meredith Charpentier, Anne Dunn, Dana Hayward, Fumi Kosaka, Marisa Miller, Rachel Orr, and Katherine Rogers. I would also like to thank David Black, Joy Tutela, and Alix Reid for their friendship, assistance, and great ideas. My wife, Joann, and my children, Jenny and Colin, are always a source of inspiration, joy, and support. Without them, I could not do my work.

I especially thank April Prince for her devoted efforts and unique contributions. This book would not have been possible without her tireless work, imagination, and creativity.

The excerpt on page 46 is from A GIRL FROM YAMHILL: A MEMOIR © 1988 by Beverly Cleary. Used with the permission of HarperCollins Publishers.

ISBN 0-439-43851-9

12 11 10 9 8 7 6 5 4 3 2 1   2 3 4 5 6 7/0

Printed in the U.S.A.   24

First Scholastic printing, September 2002

Design by Charles Yuen

Answers to quiz on back cover: 1) California, 2) Rhode Island, 3) Alaska, 4) Virginia, 5) Delaware, 6) Hawaii, 7) New York, 8) Utah, 9) Oklahoma, 10) Florida

Look at the American flag. Some people call it Old Glory. Others call it the Stars and Stripes. What do you see?

Fifty white stars. That's easy: one for each state. But there are only thirteen stripes. Why? Those red and white stripes stand for the thirteen states that made up the United States of America in 1776, the year that America was born. And you thought thirteen was an unlucky number!

Those stripes tell us that the United States of America was not always such a big place. Our country began more than two hundred years ago, when the thirteen places we now call states were still called colonies ruled by the King of England.

The thirteen separate states agreed to stand together as one nation to help one another. That is how our country got its name—the United States of America. The U.S.A. has changed a great deal during the past two centuries. Over the years more states were added. That is called being "admitted to the Union," just like getting an admission ticket to the movies. Only the states didn't have to buy a ticket.

Don't Know Much About® the 50 States tells the story of each of those states. But this book is not just filled with dates of admission and names of capitals. Like every *Don't Know Much About®* book, it is loaded with questions and answers about unusual people and places that make learning about the states a lot of fun.

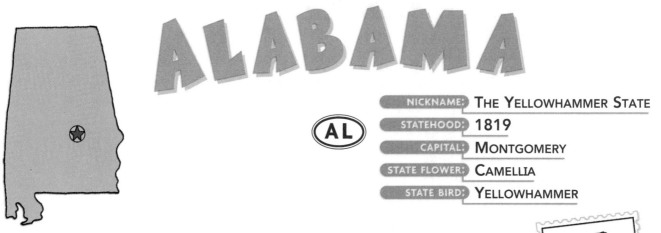

ALABAMA

AL

NICKNAME: THE YELLOWHAMMER STATE
STATEHOOD: 1819
CAPITAL: MONTGOMERY
STATE FLOWER: CAMELLIA
STATE BIRD: YELLOWHAMMER

What do Alabama's nickname and state bird have to do with the Civil War?

Alabama is called the Yellowhammer State because during the Civil War, many of the state's soldiers wore bright yellow uniforms. (Not very good camouflage, huh?) The yellowhammer was chosen as the state bird because it is the same color as those uniforms.

Camellia

Yellowhammer

Where should you go if you want to feel out of this world?

To Space Camp in Huntsville! There you can learn about space missions and feel what it's like to tumble around weightless in space. The space rocket that first sent people to the moon was invented at the Alabama Space and Rocket Center at Huntsville.

Where did Rosa Parks purposely park herself, in protest?

Alabama gets its name from a Choctaw Indian word that means "vegetation gatherers."

In 1955 Rosa Parks was arrested for sitting in an empty seat on a bus in Montgomery. The seat was for white people only, and Parks is black. Her courage started a yearlong boycott during which black people refused to ride buses. Eventually they won the right to sit wherever they wanted.

ALASKA

NICKNAME:	THE LAST FRONTIER
STATEHOOD:	1959
CAPITAL:	JUNEAU
STATE FLOWER:	FORGET-ME-NOT
STATE BIRD:	WILLOW PTARMIGAN

Willow ptarmigan

Forget-me-not

What could you do with 425 Rhode Islands?

Fit them inside Alaska! Alaska is America's largest state. If you put it on top of the lower forty-eight states, it would stretch all the way from California to Florida. Not only is it the largest state, but it also has the highest mountain (Mount McKinley), the northernmost point in the United States (Point Barrow), and the most coastline of any state. It's no wonder "Alaska" comes from an Aleutian (Eskimo) word, *alakshak*, meaning "great land"!

Alaska is closer to Russia (two miles away at one point) than it is to the rest of the United States (five hundred miles away).

Where in Alaska is it daytime—at night?

Way up in the northern parts of the state, it's light out for twenty hours a day. Just think—in the Land of the Midnight Sun, you could play a baseball game in the middle of the night, in broad daylight! In the winter, though, it's just the opposite—it's dark for twenty hours a day and light for only a few hours.

How can you travel two thousand miles across frozen Alaska without a motor?

By sled-dog! The Iditarod, Alaska's famous annual sled-dog race, is a really tough trek across Alaska that can take twenty days to finish. (If you finish it at all, that is.)

ARIZONA (AZ)

NICKNAME: THE GRAND CANYON STATE
STATEHOOD: 1912
CAPITAL: PHOENIX
STATE FLOWER: BLOSSOM OF THE SAGUARO CACTUS
STATE BIRD: CACTUS WREN

Saguaro cactus blossom

Cactus wren

Where in Arizona can you travel through two billion years of Earth's history in a single day?

Here's a hint: President Teddy Roosevelt called it "the one great sight every American should see." The answer is the Grand Canyon. The Grand Canyon is 277 miles long, up to 18 miles wide, and more than a mile deep. From the bottom, you can see how the earth was formed by looking at the layers of rock along the canyon's walls.

Who said, "I never do wrong without a cause!"?

Geronimo, an Apache warrior. When white settlers began moving west in the 1850s, Arizona's Apache Indians fought hard to keep their land. One Apache warrior named Geronimo led so many successful attacks that the United States government considered him its chief enemy and offered a $25,000 reward for his capture. After more than thirty years of fighting, Geronimo finally surrendered in 1886 and lived the rest of his life on reservations in Florida and Oklahoma.

Some people say that the cry "Geronimo!" comes from a time when the United States cavalry chased Geronimo to the edge of a cliff. The only way for Geronimo to escape was by jumping off the cliff. The warrior did just that, calling out his name as he fell safely into the river below.

Geronimo?!

ARKANSAS

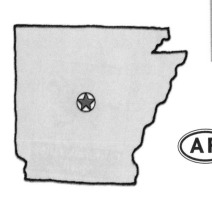

Mockingbird

NICKNAME: **THE LAND OF OPPORTUNITY**
STATEHOOD: **1836**
CAPITAL: **LITTLE ROCK**
STATE FLOWER: **APPLE BLOSSOM**
STATE BIRD: **MOCKINGBIRD**

True or false: If you find a diamond at Arkansas's Crater of Diamonds State Park, you get to keep it.

True! Crater of Diamonds, near Murfreesboro, is the only diamond mine in North America. The park is open to the public, and its diamonds are finders-keepers. Two or three diamonds are found each day (though they usually aren't the kind you'd use to make jewelry).

Did you know that Arkansas has a fountain of youth?

Well, not really, but Hot Springs National Park does have forty-seven natural springs. Some people believe the springs will make sick people well. You can bathe in the park's bathhouses but not in the springs themselves, since some of them are as hot as 147 degrees!

Apple blossom

How can you find out if you're pronouncing "Arkansas" correctly?

Ask the state legislature. In 1881 it passed a law about how to say the state's name: it's pronounced "ARK-an-saw"—the final *s* is silent.

CALIFORNIA

CA

NICKNAME:	THE GOLDEN STATE
STATEHOOD:	1850
CAPITAL:	SACRAMENTO
STATE FLOWER:	GOLDEN POPPY
STATE BIRD:	CALIFORNIA VALLEY QUAIL

California valley quail

Golden poppy

What golden opportunity in 1849 helped California earn its nickname?

Gold was discovered in 1848, and by the next year, many thousands of "forty-niners" came to get rich in the great California Gold Rush of 1849. (Get it? Forty-niners—1849.)

Did you know that California is home to:

- the tallest waterfalls in North America: Yosemite Falls

- the lowest point in the United States, Death Valley, the site of America's highest known temperature—144 degrees.

- the tallest trees on Earth: redwood trees

- the biggest trees on Earth (it would take about twenty-five of your friends holding hands to reach all the way around one tree): giant sequoia trees

Golden State Trivia

Match these California features with the places you'll find them:

1. More TV and movie studios than anywhere else in the world

2. Fossils of plants, birds, and animals stuck in oil and tar since the Ice Age

3. The Golden Gate Bridge (which really is red!)

4. Tons of computer companies

A. San Francisco

B. Silicon Valley

C. La Brea Tar Pits

D. Hollywood

COLORADO 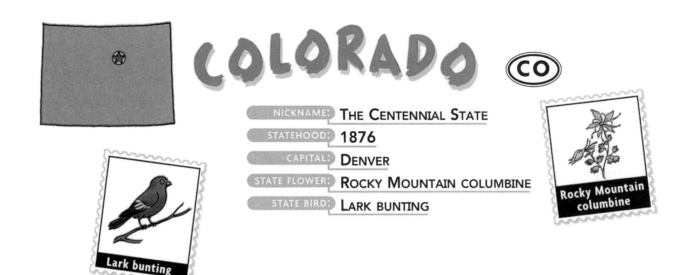 CO

NICKNAME:	THE CENTENNIAL STATE
STATEHOOD:	1876
CAPITAL:	DENVER
STATE FLOWER:	ROCKY MOUNTAIN COLUMBINE
STATE BIRD:	LARK BUNTING

Lark bunting

Rocky Mountain columbine

What does the Continental Divide divide?

It divides the continent of North America into rivers that run east and empty into the Atlantic Ocean and those that run west and empty into the Pacific Ocean. The Continental Divide runs through the Colorado Rockies.

Why are Coloradans such good sports?

The higher you are above sea level, the thinner the air gets. So, if you throw or hit a ball in Colorado's Rocky Mountains, it will go farther than at lower elevations. All that height is good for sports!

O beautiful for spacious skies,

For amber waves of grain,

For purple mountain majesties

Above the fruited plain!

Did you know that "purple mountain majesties" refers to Colorado's Rocky Mountains? "America the Beautiful" was written by an English professor named Katharine Lee Bates when she picnicked at the top of Colorado's Pikes Peak in 1893. The poem was later set to music.

CONNECTICUT

CT

Mountain laurel

Robin

NICKNAME: THE CONSTITUTION STATE
STATEHOOD: 1788
CAPITAL: HARTFORD
STATE FLOWER: MOUNTAIN LAUREL
STATE BIRD: ROBIN

What Revolutionary War hero born in Connecticut disguised himself as a schoolteacher so he could spy on the British?

Twenty-one-year-old Nathan Hale was hanged by the British in 1776 for spying. He is remembered for the phrase, "I only regret that I have but one life to lose for my country." Connecticut was also home to General Benedict Arnold, America's most infamous Revolutionary War traitor. Arnold was caught plotting to hand over the American fort at West Point to the British. He fled to England before he could be hanged.

Why is Connecticut called The Constitution State if the United States Constitution was actually written in Pennsylvania?

When Connecticut's settlers started to form the colony in 1634, they soon adopted the Fundamental Orders, which many people consider the first written American constitution. The orders gave people who voted the right to choose who ran the government.

A constitution lists the basic laws and rules of a country. The United States Constitution was adopted in 1787.

15

DELAWARE

NICKNAME: THE FIRST STATE

STATEHOOD: 1787

CAPITAL: DOVER

STATE FLOWER: PEACH BLOSSOM

STATE BIRD: BLUE HEN CHICKEN

DE

Blue hen chicken

Peach blossom

What did Delaware do before any of the other states?

It approved the United States Constitution, thus earning one of its nicknames—the First State. Thomas Jefferson said Delaware was like a diamond, "small, but valuable." (The Diamond State, another of Delaware's nicknames, is indeed small; it's only nine miles wide at its narrowest!)

:-)

What did Dela wear to the ball?

Ida ho, Al aska.

Delaware is the name of

(a) a river

(b) a group of Indians

(c) a state

(d) all of the above

If you answered d, all of the above, you win a Delaware Blue hen! (The Delaware Blue hen was actually a favorite breed of chicken raised in the state more than 200 years ago.) The state was named after the Delaware Indians, only *Delaware* isn't an Indian word at all. British explorers gave this name to the Lenni-Lenape Indian tribe because they lived near the Delaware River, but the river itself was named after Virginia governor Thomas West, Lord De La Warr. (Get it? De-la-ware.) He had never even seen the area.

FLORIDA (FL)

NICKNAME: THE SUNSHINE STATE
STATEHOOD: 1845
CAPITAL: TALLAHASSEE
STATE FLOWER: ORANGE BLOSSOM
STATE BIRD: MOCKINGBIRD

Orange blossom

Mockingbird

Where can Americans go from Cape Canaveral that they can't go from anywhere else in the United States?

Outer space! The John F. Kennedy Space Center is the launching pad for American space missions. From that base:

- astronaut Alan Shepard became the first American in space, in 1961;
- John Glenn became the first American to orbit the Earth, in 1962;
- Neil Armstrong became the first man to walk on the moon, in 1969.

Visitors to the Space Center can sit in a lunar rover, learn how astronauts prepare to go into space, and try on a spacesuit. Blast off!

Florida's threatened and endangered animals include:

(a) American crocodiles

(b) bald eagles

(c) manatees

(d) Florida panthers

(e) all of the above

The answer is, sadly, e. Some of the rarest plants and animals in the country live in Florida's Everglades, one of the world's largest swamps, which is itself endangered.

KNOCK, KNOCK!

Who's there?

Orange.

Orange who?

Orange you going to ask about Florida oranges?

Because of the Sunshine State's sunny climate, Florida grows more citrus fruit (oranges, grapefruit, lemons) than any other state.

GEORGIA

NICKNAME:	THE PEACH STATE
STATEHOOD:	1788
CAPITAL:	ATLANTA
STATE FLOWER:	CHEROKEE ROSE
STATE BIRD:	BROWN THRASHER

GA

Brown thrasher

Cherokee rose

If Georgia is old enough to be the fourth state, why are there so few old buildings in Atlanta, its capital?

Poor Atlanta. At the end of the Civil War, Union general William T. Sherman ordered Atlanta to be burned because the Confederates' food and guns were stored there. The city had to be rebuilt from the ground up.

When cola syrup was accidentally mixed with carbonated water and served at Jacobs' Pharmacy in Atlanta in 1886, Coca-Cola was born. Today its secret recipe is known by only two men, who try never to travel together—just in case there's an accident. . . .

Ever heard of goobers?

If you're not from the South, you probably haven't. Here are a few hints: they're what locals call the main ingredient in peanut butter, and they come salted in the shell, honey roasted, and in Snickers bars. Georgia grows more . . . *peanuts* than any other state.

What Georgian was King of the civil rights movement?

The Reverend Dr. Martin Luther King, Jr., was America's most famous civil rights leader. King led nonviolent protests to fight for social and political rights for African Americans and others. In his hometown of Atlanta an eternal flame burns to honor his memory.

18

HAWAII

Yellow hibiscus

(HI)

NICKNAME:	THE ALOHA STATE
STATEHOOD:	1959
CAPITAL:	HONOLULU
STATE FLOWER:	YELLOW HIBISCUS
STATE BIRD:	NENE (HAWAIIAN GOOSE)

What is Hawaii, exactly?

Hawaii is both a state and an island. The state of Hawaii is made up of 132 islands, but only eight are big enough to live on. The well-known Hawaiian islands are Maui, Oahu, Kauai, and, of course, Hawaii, called the Big Island. Hawaii is the southernmost place in the United States, and is about two thousand miles from California in the Pacific Ocean.

How does the island of Hawaii grow larger each year?

Each time Mauna Loa—one of the world's largest active volcanoes—erupts, the lava cools and hardens in the ocean, making the island bigger. This is how all the Hawaiian islands were formed, but the volcanoes on the other islands are no longer active.

Nene

The only royal palace in America is Hawaii's Iolani Palace. Hawaii was ruled by kings and queens from 1795 until 1893.

The Hawaiian word *aloha* means:

(a) hello

(b) good-bye

(c) love

(d) friendship

(e) all of the above

The answer is e. What a happy word!

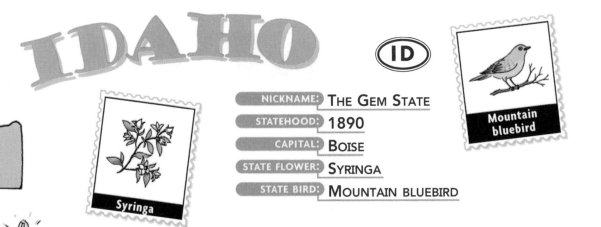

IDAHO

ID

NICKNAME: **THE GEM STATE**

STATEHOOD: 1890

CAPITAL: BOISE

STATE FLOWER: SYRINGA

STATE BIRD: MOUNTAIN BLUEBIRD

Syringa

Mountain bluebird

What precious things can you find in Idaho?

Precious stones! The Gem State produces more than eighty different kinds of precious stones, including opals, garnets, sapphires, and rubies.

How do astronauts walk on the moon while keeping their feet on the earth?

NASA astronauts used to practice for missions at Craters of the Moon National Park because the land there looks so much like the land on the moon. The park has many colors of volcanic lava that has hardened into strange, twisted shapes. There are lots of caves and eerie holes in the ground that steam rises out of, too.

:-)

What peels and chips but doesn't crack?

A potato!

"Dice 'em, hash 'em, boil 'em, mash 'em! Idaho! Idaho! Idaho!" What does this Idaho football cheer refer to?

Potatoes, of course! If all the potatoes grown in the state in a year were put end to end, they'd stretch more than two million miles—or to the moon and back eight times! There would be one hundred and twenty potatoes for each person in America. That's a lot of french fries!

ILLINOIS

NICKNAME: **THE PRAIRIE STATE**
STATEHOOD: **1818**
CAPITAL: **SPRINGFIELD**
STATE FLOWER: **NATIVE VIOLET**
STATE BIRD: **CARDINAL**

IL

Cardinal

What heated up Illinois in 1871?

The great Chicago fire, which rapidly spread through the entire city. The city's wooden houses fed the fire, which burned for more than twenty-four hours and left at least 250 people dead and 100,000 homeless. One good thing came out of the fire, however: Many talented architects helped rebuild the city, which became known for its beautiful and interesting buildings.

Native violet

What skyscraper is the tallest building in North America?

The Sears Tower in Chicago, which is 110 stories high. The tower was the tallest office building in the world when it was built in 1974. Since then, a slightly taller one was built in Kuala Lumpur, Malaysia. You can ride to the top of the Sears Tower in one of the fastest elevators in the world, and on a clear day you can see Wisconsin, Michigan, and Indiana from the top.

Chicago's O'Hare airport is the busiest airport in the world. A plane takes off or lands every 23 seconds.

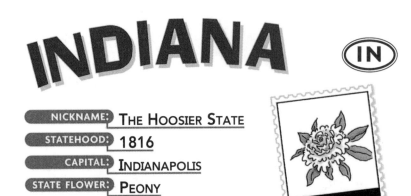

INDIANA

NICKNAME:	THE HOOSIER STATE
STATEHOOD:	1816
CAPITAL:	INDIANAPOLIS
STATE FLOWER:	PEONY
STATE BIRD:	CARDINAL

Peony

Cardinal

Garfield creator Jim Davis, basketball star Larry Bird, and singer Michael Jackson are all famous Hoosiers. No one is quite sure why Indiana is called the Hoosier State, but the nickname may come from an early pioneer greeting, "Who'shyer?" meaning "Who's there?" or "How are you?"

Indiana, or *Indian* plus *a*, means "land of Indians." The Illinois, Shawnee, Miami, and other Native American tribes lived here before the settlers arrived.

KNOCK, KNOCK!

Who's there?
Hoosier.
Hoosier who?
Hoosier favorite Hoosier?

If the race car drivers in the Indianapolis 500 drive around the track only 200 times, why is the race called the Indianapolis 500?

The track is 2½ miles long, so the 200 laps make for 500 miles. The drivers go as fast as 237 miles per hour! (That's about three times as fast as your parents drive on the highway.) The race, held each Memorial Day, draws more fans than any other sports event—up to four times as many as the Superbowl.

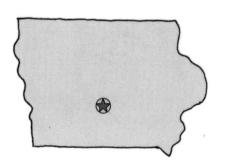

Eastern goldfinch

IOWA

IA

If you're driving through Iowa, what will you see out your window?

Wild rose

Farms, farms, and more farms. Farmland makes up about 95 percent of the state. Iowa is also known as the Corn State because it grows more corn than any other state (except sometimes Illinois). Bet it doesn't surprise you that Iowa is home to the biggest popcorn factory in the country.

Ears an interesting fact about Iowa corn: it can grow as high as thirty feet tall! (That's about equal to you and six friends standing on each other's shoulders!)

"I loved my towns, my cornfields, and the home of my people. I fought for it. It is now yours. Keep it as we did. It will produce you good crops."

Black Hawk, —Sauk Indian Chief

Why is Iowa called the Hawkeye State?

Iowa was nicknamed the Hawkeye State in honor of the Indian chief Black Hawk, who was forced to give up his land after the Black Hawk War of 1832. *Iowa* is an Iowa Indian word that means "this is the place" or "the beautiful land."

KANSAS (KS)

NICKNAME:	THE SUNFLOWER STATE
STATEHOOD:	1861
CAPITAL:	TOPEKA
STATE FLOWER:	SUNFLOWER
STATE BIRD:	WESTERN MEADOWLARK

What took Dorothy and Toto away from their Kansas home?

A tornado. Kansas gets lots of tornadoes. This kind of powerful, swirling storm took Dorothy and her dog to the wonderful Land of Oz. The name "Kansas" comes from the Sioux word *kansa*, meaning "people of the wind."

"The night I flew over the Pacific was a night of stars. They seemed to rise from the sea and hang outside my cockpit window, near enough to touch."

—**Amelia Earhart**

Sunflower

Western meadowlark

What Kansan set an aviation record?

Airplane pilot Amelia Earhart, who was born in Kansas, was the first woman to fly alone across the Atlantic Ocean, in 1932. In 1937 Earhart mysteriously disappeared over the Pacific Ocean while trying to fly around the world.

KENTUCKY

(KY)

NICKNAME:	THE BLUEGRASS STATE
STATEHOOD:	1792
CAPITAL:	FRANKFORT
STATE FLOWER:	GOLDENROD
STATE BIRD:	KENTUCKY CARDINAL

Kentucky cardinal

Goldenrod

Does the Bluegrass State really have blue grass?

The grass in Kentucky isn't *really* blue, but it does bloom with blue flowers in the spring. The state's thigh-slapping, toe-tapping folk music is also called bluegrass.

Where in Kentucky can you find eyeless fish and blind beetles?

In the darkest parts of Kentucky's Mammoth Caves, the largest cave system in the whole world. The caves have more than three hundred miles of underground passages, lakes, rivers, and waterfalls (underground waterfalls!)—and that only includes the parts that have been explored.

Most of the United States gold reserve—more than $40 billion—is kept at Kentucky's Fort Knox.

What Kentucky race is known as "the most exciting two minutes in sports"?

The Kentucky Derby, America's oldest yearly horse race, held each May at Louisville's Churchill Downs. Kentucky is famous for its champion racehorses.

LOUISIANA

NICKNAME:	THE PELICAN STATE
STATEHOOD:	1812
CAPITAL:	BATON ROUGE
STATE FLOWER:	MAGNOLIA
STATE BIRD:	EASTERN BROWN PELICAN

Eastern brown pelican

LA

Magnolia

Why is the Pelican State also called the Sportsman's Paradise?

Louisiana is home to lots of pelicans. Pelicans love to catch fish, and Louisiana is a great place for sportsmen to do the same. With the Mississippi River, the Gulf of Mexico, and all of the state's swamps and bayous (*BI-yooz*), Louisiana makes more money from fishing than any other state. The Fisherman's Paradise exports shrimp, oysters, and frogs, and much of the world's crayfish.

What musician made New Orleans famous as "the cradle of jazz"?

Jazz, a kind of music that combines music from Africa and the American South, started in New Orleans in the early 1900s. Around the same time, a young musician named Louis Armstrong was singing for pennies on the streets and playing a guitar he had made out of a cigar box. Armstrong eventually helped make jazz famous with his trumpet playing and unique singing voice.

A bayou is what Louisianans call a stream or creek. Bayous are often marshy, shallow, and full of fish and wild animals to hunt.

MAINE

NICKNAME: THE PINE TREE STATE

STATEHOOD: 1820

CAPITAL: AUGUSTA

STATE FLOWER: WHITE PINE CONE AND TASSEL

STATE BIRD: CHICKADEE

White pine cone and tassel

(ME)

Strain your brain on Maine: Which of the following are true?

(a) It's the only state whose name has only one syllable.

(b) Lions with thick, bushy *manes* live in the state.

(c) French explorers might have named it after a region in France called *Mayne*.

(d) The state is the *main* place in America for lighthouses, lobster, and wild blueberries.

If you guessed a, c, and d, you're right! As for the lions . . . you'll have to head to Africa, or to the zoo!

Chickadee

If you live in West Quoddy Head, Maine, what do you get to do before anyone else in the United States, every single day of every year?

See the sun rise! West Quoddy Head is farther east than any other place on the East Coast of the United States. Now, quick: Do you remember which state is the farthest south? If not, unscramble these letters—AIWHAI— or turn to page 19 to find out!

MARYLAND

(MD)

NICKNAME: THE OLD LINE STATE
STATEHOOD: 1788
CAPITAL: ANNAPOLIS
STATE FLOWER: BLACK-EYED SUSAN
STATE BIRD: BALTIMORE ORIOLE

Baltimore oriole

Black-eyed Susan

What's the key to remembering who wrote our National Anthem?

The fact that the poet's last name is Key! In 1814 Francis Scott Key wrote "The Star-Spangled Banner." He was inspired by a twenty-five-hour battle between the Americans and the British during the War of 1812. As Key watched the battle at Fort McHenry from a sailboat in Baltimore harbor, he kept his eye out for the American flag. He knew that as long as the Stars and Stripes flew, the Americans had not been defeated. When the battle was over, he wrote his famous words on the back of a letter he happened to have in his pocket. The poem, later set to music, was to become the national anthem of the United States.

Was the Underground Railroad the first subway system?

"I was a conductor on the Underground Railroad for eight years, and I can say what most conductors can't say—I never ran my train off the track and I never lost a passenger."

—Abolitionist Harriet Tubman

It sure sounds like it, but the Underground Railroad was really a series of houses and other safe places for slaves who were running away to freedom before the Civil War. Abolitionists (people who were against slavery) helped the slaves move north from one station along the "railroad" to another, usually at night. Harriet Tubman, herself an escaped slave who grew up in Maryland, became one of the most famous "conductors" of the Underground Railroad and helped at least three hundred other slaves escape.

MASSACHUSETTS

Mayflower

NICKNAME:	THE BAY STATE
STATEHOOD:	1788
CAPITAL:	BOSTON
STATE FLOWER:	MAYFLOWER
STATE BIRD:	CHICKADEE

MA

Chickadee

Was Massachusetts the site of the first British colony in America?

It seems like it should be, because we learn so much about the Pilgrims and their first Thanksgiving. But Plymouth, where the Pilgrims landed, was actually the second permanent British colony in America. Jamestown, Virginia, was the first, in 1607.

Where was Paul Revere going on his famous midnight ride?

On April 18, 1775, the night before the first battles of the American Revolution, Paul Revere left Boston on horseback for Lexington and Concord. It's a good thing he wasn't the only rider carrying the message that the British were coming, because Revere was captured just as he left Lexington. One of the other patriots, Samuel Prescott, made it to Concord.

The first Thanksgiving was held in October, not November, and lasted for three days!

Why is Massachusetts the best place for little women to eat green eggs and ham?

Because both Louisa May Alcott, author of *Little Women*, and Theodor Geisel (better known as Dr. Seuss!) were born here. Other famous authors include Emily Dickinson, Ralph Waldo Emerson, and Edgar Allan Poe.

MICHIGAN

Robin

Apple blossom

NICKNAME:	THE WOLVERINE STATE
STATEHOOD:	1837
CAPITAL:	LANSING
STATE FLOWER:	APPLE BLOSSOM
STATE BIRD:	ROBIN

MI

Michigan is broken into two separate pieces of land. Its Upper and Lower Peninsulas touch four of the five Great Lakes: Erie, Huron, Michigan, and Superior. With all the nooks and crannies, this gives the state a shoreline of 3,100 miles! The name "Michigan" comes from two Chippewa Indian words, *mici* and *gama*, that together mean "great water."

What product of Detroit is this 1901 advertisement promoting?

"Travels rough roads smoothly. A child can operate it safely. Speed up to 25 miles per hour without fear of breakdown. Goes 40 miles on one gallon of gasoline."

A "horseless carriage" (a car). Detroit is often called "Motor City" or "Motortown" because it makes more cars than any other city in the world.

How did Motown music get its name?

Detroit is also famous for its music, "Motown" (short for Motortown), which combines pop and black gospel music. If you've ever heard the song "Stop! In the Name of Love" by the Supremes, then you know what Motown sounds like.

If you want to remember the names of the five Great Lakes, just remember the word HOMES, for: Huron, Ontario, Michigan, Erie, Superior.

MINNESOTA

NICKNAME:	THE LAND OF 10,000 LAKES
STATEHOOD:	1858
CAPITAL:	ST. PAUL
STATE FLOWER:	PINK AND WHITE LADY'S SLIPPER
STATE BIRD:	COMMON LOON

Common loon

Pink and white lady's slipper

Are there really 10,000 lakes in Minnesota?

Actually, there are at least 15,000, and maybe more than 22,000. There are so many lakes in Minnesota that people ran out of names and started using old names over again! There are 201 Mud Lakes, 154 Long Lakes, 123 Rice Lakes, and 83 Bass Lakes.

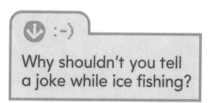

:-)

Why shouldn't you tell a joke while ice fishing?

The ice might crack up!

What Minnesotan was so big that he used a pine tree to brush his beard?

Of all tall-tale heroes, Paul Bunyan was probably the tallest. In the 1800s loggers told stories about the huge imaginary lumberjack who lived in Minnesota with his blue ox, Babe. Legend has it that each of Paul's enormous footprints became one of Minnesota's lakes.

MISSISSIPPI

NICKNAME: **The Magnolia State**
STATEHOOD: **1817**
CAPITAL: **Jackson**
STATE FLOWER: **Magnolia**
STATE BIRD: **Mockingbird**

MS

Mockingbird

Magnolia

:-)
What has four eyes but can't see?

Mississippi.

Of the ten states that border the Mississippi River, why was the state of Mississippi the one to be named after it?

No other state had taken the name yet! The name of this state, and the largest river in America, most likely comes from two Chippewa Indian words, *mici* and *zibi*, meaning "father of the waters." The rich, dark soil deposited by the river is some of the best in the world for growing crops.

What do you get when you combine a marionette and a puppet?

Grover, Oscar the Grouch, Miss Piggy, Kermit the Frog—Muppets! The Muppets' creator, Jim Henson, grew up in Leland and named Kermit after one of his childhood friends.

MISSOURI

NICKNAME: THE SHOW ME STATE
STATEHOOD: 1821
CAPITAL: JEFFERSON CITY
STATE FLOWER: HAWTHORN
STATE BIRD: BLUEBIRD

MO

Bluebird

Hawthorn

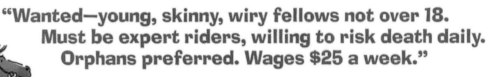
"Wanted—young, skinny, wiry fellows not over 18. Must be expert riders, willing to risk death daily. Orphans preferred. Wages $25 a week."

If you answered this ad from an 1860 Missouri newspaper, you'd be hoping to ride for the Pony Express, an early mail service that carried letters from St. Joseph, Missouri, to Sacramento, California, before America's cross-country telegraph lines were connected.

Brave riders rode on horseback at top speed, even in snow or through the desert, to cover the two thousand miles in just ten days.

Missouri is one of only two states to border eight other states: Iowa, Illinois, Kentucky, Tennessee, Arkansas, Oklahoma, Kansas, and Nebraska. Which of these states also touches eight states? Hint: It's the only one that has more letters in its name than the number of states it touches.

Answer: Tennessee

"There comes a time in every rightly constructed boy's life when he has a raging desire to go somewhere and dig for hidden treasure."

—The Adventures of Tom Sawyer

In Mark Twain's book, Tom and his friend Huck Finn decide to become pirates on the Mississippi River. Twain (whose real name was Samuel Langhorne Clemens) grew up in Hannibal and later was a riverboat pilot on the Mississippi.

MONTANA

NICKNAME:	THE TREASURE STATE
STATEHOOD:	1889
CAPITAL:	HELENA
STATE FLOWER:	BITTERROOT
STATE BIRD:	WESTERN MEADOWLARK

(MT)

Western meadowlark

Bitterroot

Have pirates been hiding out in Montana?

Without a coast, Montana hasn't been visited by any pirates, but the state does have buried treasure of another kind. Gold, silver, copper, and zinc are all mined in the Treasure State, which also produces more sapphires than any other state.

Who was left standing at Custer's Last Stand?

The Sioux and Cheyenne warriors, led by Crazy Horse. Custer's Last Stand, also known as the Battle of Little Bighorn, in 1876 was the Indians' last and largest victory during the Plains Indian Wars. Lieutenant Colonel George A. Custer thought he was so powerful that he paid no attention to warnings that his army would be greatly outnumbered. In the space of just one hour, Custer and all his men lost their lives. His defeat embarrassed and angered the American government, causing it to fight the Indians even harder.

Montana, called Big Sky Country, has set aside twenty-five million acres of land on which elk, grizzly bears, mountain lions, and buffalo are free to roam. The state also has lots of sheep and cattle ranches: In Montana, cows outnumber people by about three to one.

NEBRASKA

NE

Goldenrod

NICKNAME:	THE CORNHUSKER STATE
STATEHOOD:	1867
CAPITAL:	LINCOLN
STATE FLOWER:	GOLDENROD
STATE BIRD:	WESTERN MEADOWLARK

Why were Nebraska's first settlers called "sodbusters"?

There may not have been many trees in Nebraska when the first settlers arrived, but there *was* a lot of grass. So settlers made their houses out of sod, or thin layers of dirt and grass, which they cut, or "busted," into blocks.

What national holiday has its roots in Nebraska?

Arbor Day, a holiday for planting trees, was started in 1872 in then almost treeless Nebraska by a man named J. Sterling Morton. Morton knew that trees would enable people to build houses and barns, help protect people from floods and blizzards, and make the soil more fertile. The Nebraska National Forest is the only national forest planted solely by people.

Nebraska is the only state to take its nickname from a college mascot, the University of Nebraska's Cornhusker. (The university took the name from the state's main agricultural product and from the cornhusking contests farmers used to hold.)

Western meadowlark

NEVADA

NICKNAME:	THE SILVER STATE
STATEHOOD:	1864
CAPITAL:	CARSON CITY
STATE FLOWER:	SAGEBRUSH
STATE BIRD:	MOUNTAIN BLUEBIRD

Sagebrush

Mountain bluebird

To build Nevada's Hoover Dam, concrete was poured continually for:

(a) one day

(c) two years

(b) three months

(d) ten years

The answer is c: two years! The 726-foot-high Hoover Dam gives water to local farms and electricity to Nevada, Arizona, and southern California. The dam created Lake Mead, the largest man-made lake in the United States and one of the largest in the world.

What Nevada city am I?

- With all my neon lights and air-conditioning, I have the highest electric bills per person in America.

- I am the live entertainment capital of the world.

- Four hundred couples get married in me every day.

- I am home to more than fifty casinos, where people try their luck at cards, dice, and other games of chance.

I'm Las Vegas!

NEW HAMPSHIRE

(NH)

Purple finch

NICKNAME:	THE GRANITE STATE
STATEHOOD:	1788
CAPITAL:	CONCORD
STATE FLOWER:	PURPLE LILAC
STATE BIRD:	PURPLE FINCH

Did you know it?
New Hampshire's a prizewinning poet!

Well, the Pulitzer Prize for poetry didn't actually go to the state, it went to Robert Frost for his book called *New Hampshire*. Robert Frost was born in San Francisco but later settled on a farm in New Hampshire. Frost is famous for his many poems about New England and its people. In a poem called "New Hampshire," Frost says the state is one of the two best in America. (The other being New Hampshire's next-door neighbor, Vermont, where he was living at the time!)

Purple lilac

Why is New Hampshire sometimes known as the "state that made the nation"?

Nine of the original thirteen colonies needed to approve the Constitution for the United States to become a nation. New Hampshire was the ninth to do so. New Hampshirites also were the first colonists to declare their independence from England: they formed their own government in January 1776—six months before the Declaration of Independence was signed!

The Library of Congress in Washington, D.C., is made from New Hampshire's granite, a hard gray rock that lies under much of the state.

If you go to Mount Washington, hold on to your hat! A wind of 231 miles per hour, the strongest wind ever recorded in the United States, blew across it in 1934.

NEW JERSEY

NICKNAME: THE GARDEN STATE

STATEHOOD: 1787

CAPITAL: TRENTON

STATE FLOWER: PURPLE VIOLET

STATE BIRD: EASTERN GOLDFINCH

NJ

Eastern goldfinch

Purple violet

If New Jersey has so many smokestacks and factories, why is it called the Garden State?

New Jersey does have lots of factories and more people per square mile than any other state, but the Garden State also has sandy beaches and beautiful farmland. During the American Revolution, New Jersey farms provided much of the food the soldiers needed to win the war. Today the state grows food for nearby Philadelphia and New York City.

What famous inventor, known as the "Wizard of Menlo Park," had only three months of formal schooling?

Thomas Edison invented the movie camera, the electric lightbulb, the phonograph, even wax paper—all told, over 1,093 inventions in his lifetime. When Edison opened his factory in Menlo Park in 1876, he said it would produce "a minor invention every ten days and a big thing every six months or so." And it did!

If you're strolling down Atlantic Avenue, the Boardwalk, and Park Place, are you in a life-sized game of Monopoly?

No, you're in Atlantic City. The spaces of the board game Monopoly are named after its streets.

NEW MEXICO

(NM)

NICKNAME: THE LAND OF ENCHANTMENT
STATEHOOD: 1912
CAPITAL: SANTA FE
STATE FLOWER: YUCCA
STATE BIRD: ROADRUNNER

Yucca

Roadrunner

If New Mexico is "new," how can it be so old?

Spanish explorers named the area New Mexico way back in 1540, when they first came north from Mexico. In many parts of the state, you can see pottery with designs that can be traced back more than two thousand years, to the Anasazi Indians.

Why do many buildings in New Mexico look different from those in other states?

Many buildings in New Mexico are made of *adobe* bricks, or blocks of clay and straw that have been dried in the sun. People who live in the desert have built adobe houses for hundreds of years because these houses stay cool in the heat, and wood was not available. In Taos you can find one of New Mexico's oldest adobe *pueblos*, or villages, built more than 700 years ago. Today, the state is known for its unique mix of Indian, Spanish, and American traditions.

What New Mexico cave might drive you batty?

Carlsbad Caverns in southeastern New Mexico are the deepest limestone caves in the world. Every night, thousands of bats fly out of the caves and return before morning.

NEW YORK

NICKNAME: THE EMPIRE STATE

STATEHOOD: 1788

CAPITAL: ALBANY

STATE FLOWER: ROSE

STATE BIRD: BLUEBIRD

Did all of New York's Manhattan Island really cost just $24?

Peter Minuit, the leader of the Dutch colony of New Amsterdam, bought Manhattan in 1626 from the Lenape Indians for $24 worth of beads, cloth, and hatchets. Today that sum would be worth about $480—which still makes the purchase a bargain! The British renamed New Amsterdam New York in 1664, for the Duke of York, Britain's future king.

I'm big, I'm green, I'm America's Welcome Queen. Who am I?

The Statue of Liberty, in New York harbor, which greeted people as they arrived by boat to settle in the United States, is technically in New Jersey. The statue, a gift from France, is still a reminder of hope and freedom—the reasons many people move to America. Today you can climb 354 steps inside her to reach the crown.

NY

Bluebird

Rose

The first stop for people entering New York harbor was Ellis Island. It was called the "Gateway to the New World" because twelve million people who wanted to move to the United States stopped at the island between 1892 and 1954. Did you know that chances are one in three that you have a relative who stopped at Ellis Island?

Beautiful Niagara Falls are actually two waterfalls. One's in New York, and the other is in Canada. Niagara Falls has inspired people to do some crazy things:

- A man named Sam Patch dove over not once, but twice, in the late 1820s.

- Schoolteacher Annie Taylor became the first to go over the falls in a barrel, in 1901. She lived, but others who tried later were not as lucky.

- French daredevil Charles Blondin crossed the falls many times on his tightrope in 1859 and 1860. Once he pushed a stove along in a wheelbarrow and halfway across cooked himself an omelet!

NORTH CAROLINA

NC

NICKNAME:	THE TAR HEEL STATE
STATEHOOD:	1789
CAPITAL:	RALEIGH
STATE FLOWER:	DOGWOOD
STATE BIRD:	CARDINAL

Cardinal

Dogwood

So what's a Tar Heel, anyway?

North Carolina's pine trees make a lot of tar—and tar, of course, is very sticky. Legend has it that during the Civil War, North Carolina soldiers stood as bravely in battle as if they had tar on their heels.

What two brothers had the Wright stuff?

Orville and Wilbur Wright brought their flying machine to Kitty Hawk, North Carolina, on December 17, 1903, because the National Weather Service said the spot was one of the windiest in North America—and they needed wind to get their airplane off the ground. The first successful powered airplane flight lasted twelve seconds, and the craft traveled about half a football field.

The first English colony in America was started on North Carolina's Roanoke Island in 1587. Just a few years after the colony was settled, though, its people mysteriously disappeared. Almost no trace of the settlers from the "Lost Colony" was found, not even skeletons.

NORTH DAKOTA

ND

NICKNAME:	THE FLICKERTAIL STATE
STATEHOOD:	1889
CAPITAL:	BISMARCK
STATE FLOWER:	WILD PRAIRIE ROSE
STATE BIRD:	WESTERN MEADOWLARK

Western meadowlark

Wild prairie rose

Why do North and South Dakota share the same name?

The two states together were once the Dakota Territory, named for a nation of Oglala, Lakota, Teton, and other Indians who called themselves Dakota, or "league of friends." The territory was made into two states because it was so large.

Who was Sacagawea?

In 1804, Meriwether Lewis and William Clark set out to explore the Louisiana Territory. Near their winter camp in Washburn, a Shoshone Indian teenager named Sacagawea joined them. (You can see her picture on the gold-colored dollar coin.) She spoke English because she had once been captured and sold to a Canadian fur trapper. Without her help as a guide and interpreter, it is doubtful that Lewis and Clark would have reached the Pacific Ocean.

"I would never have been president if it had not been for my experiences in North Dakota."
—Theodore Roosevelt

President Teddy Roosevelt spent three years on a ranch in North Dakota in the 1880s. Roosevelt is the only president to have a national park, Theodore Roosevelt National Park, in southwest North Dakota, named after him.

OHIO

OH

NICKNAME: THE BUCKEYE STATE
STATEHOOD: 1803
CAPITAL: COLUMBUS
STATE FLOWER: SCARLET CARNATION
STATE BIRD: CARDINAL

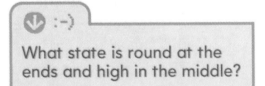

Cardinal

Scarlet carnation

How many United States presidents were born in Ohio?

Ohio sometimes is called the Mother of Modern Presidents because seven American presidents, all of whom served after the Civil War, were born there: Ulysses S. Grant, Rutherford B. Hayes, James Garfield, Benjamin Harrison, William McKinley, William Howard Taft, and Warren G. Harding.

:-)

What state is round at the ends and high in the middle?

¡O-IH-O

Why does Ohio have oodles of apple orchards?

John Chapman, better known as Johnny Appleseed, was born in Massachusetts in 1774, but he spent most of his life planting apple trees in the Ohio River valley. He gave apple seeds and seedlings to everyone he met. He loved apples, apple trees, and animals, and was a friend of the Indians. Folklore says he traveled barefoot and wore a tin pot as a hat and a coffee sack as a shirt.

OKLAHOMA

NICKNAME: THE SOONER STATE

STATEHOOD: 1907

CAPITAL: OKLAHOMA CITY

STATE FLOWER: MISTLETOE

STATE BIRD: SCISSORTAILED FLYCATCHER

Mistletoe

Scissortailed flycatcher

I'm gooey, black, and will make you rich, and I'm called Oklahoma's "black gold." What am I?

Oil! Oklahoma has so much oil underground that people have discovered oil in their backyards. There's even an oil well on the lawn of the state capitol!

Why are there more languages spoken in Oklahoma than in all of Europe?

Oklahoma is home to at least fifty-five Indian nations, each of which has its own language or dialect. Each tribe controls its own government, schools, and land. The name "Oklahoma" comes from two Choctaw Indian words: *humma* and *okla*, meaning "red people."

Were some of Oklahoma's first white settlers a little bit naughty?

At noon on April 22, 1889, the United States opened the Oklahoma Territory for settlement. A gun was fired to start the land rush . . . but some eager settlers "jumped the gun" and claimed their land early. The Sooner State gets its name from the pioneers who thought they would get better land if they got there "sooner."

Most of the Indian tribes who now live in Oklahoma were forced to walk there by the United States government during the mid-1800s. The journey became known as the Trail of Tears because so many died along the way.

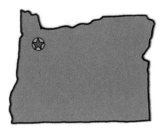

OREGON

Western meadowlark

OR

NICKNAME:	THE BEAVER STATE
STATEHOOD:	1859
CAPITAL:	SALEM
STATE FLOWER:	OREGON GRAPE
STATE BIRD:	WESTERN MEADOWLARK

Oregon grape

Were pioneers on the Oregon Trail really headed for Oregon?

The Oregon Trail was a two-thousand-mile route that pioneers followed to Oregon and other places in the West in the 1840s to the 1860s. In some places along the trail, you can still see the tracks made by the thousands of covered wagons that traveled along it more than 150 years ago.

"In the library in seventh grade . . . I found a place on the shelf where my book would be if I ever wrote a book, which I doubted."

—Beverly Cleary, A Girl from Yamhill: A Memoir

What Oregon-born author overcame her doubts and went on to create Ramona Quimby?

Beverly Cleary's stories about Ramona Quimby, Ramona's older sister, Beezus, and their neighbor, Henry Huggins, take place just outside the city of Portland.

PENNSYLVANIA

PA

NICKNAME:	THE KEYSTONE STATE
STATEHOOD:	1787
CAPITAL:	HARRISBURG
STATE FLOWER:	MOUNTAIN LAUREL
STATE BIRD:	RUFFLED GROUSE

Mountain laurel

Ruffled grouse

What is a keystone anyway?

A keystone is the stone that holds an arch together. Pennsylvania is called the Keystone State. It sat right in the middle of the colonies, and both the Declaration of Independence and the U.S. Constitution were signed at the Pennsylvania State House in Philadelphia.

You turkey!

Ben Franklin was one of America's most famous writers, leaders, and scientists. He created Philadelphia's first fire department, Pennsylvania's first university and public hospital, and the nation's first public library. But when it came to fowl, his ideas were foul! Ben wanted to make the wild turkey the national symbol, because it lived only in America and Ben thought it acted nobly. Thank goodness the bald eagle was chosen instead!

Ben Franklin started a magazine called *Poor Richard's Almanac*, which included famous Franklin sayings, such as:

"Early to bed, and early to rise, makes a man healthy, wealthy, and wise."

"Fish and visitors smell in three days."

"Three may keep a secret if two are dead."

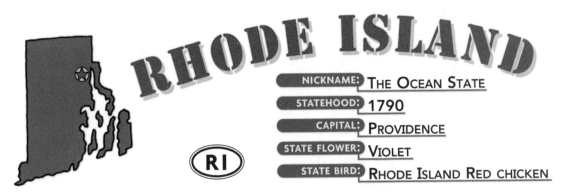

RHODE ISLAND

NICKNAME: THE OCEAN STATE
STATEHOOD: 1790
CAPITAL: PROVIDENCE
STATE FLOWER: VIOLET
STATE BIRD: RHODE ISLAND RED CHICKEN

RI

Just how small is "Little Rhody"?

It's only forty-eight miles long and thirty-seven miles wide. Do you remember how many times Rhode Island could fit inside Alaska? See page 9 for the answer! It's funny that the smallest state in the nation has the longest official name: The State of Rhode Island and Providence Plantations.

Where is the founder of Rhode Island buried?

No one knows! Rhode Island settlers were grateful for Roger Williams, who founded Rhode Island as the first colony where people could practice any religion freely. Williams and his wife were first buried on their farm in Providence. But when admiring Rhode Islanders decided to dig up the graves and give them a fancier place to rest, the graves were empty!

If you just arrived in Rhode Island, is it more likely that you rode in a car or rowed a boat to get there?

Since Rhode Island isn't really an island, you probably came by car. Rhode Island got its name from just one of the islands that is now part of the state of Rhode Island. (Today, the Ocean State is made up of thirty-six islands and one mainland.) And as for the "Rhode"? In 1524, Italian explorer Giovanni da Verrazzano said the island was about the same size as the Greek island of Rhodes. "Rhode" may also have come from the Dutch explorer Adriaen Block, who called the island *Roodt*, or red, because of its red soil.

Violet

Rhode Island Red

SOUTH CAROLINA

NICKNAME: THE PALMETTO STATE
STATEHOOD: 1788
CAPITAL: COLUMBIA
STATE FLOWER: CAROLINA JESSAMINE
STATE BIRD: CAROLINA WREN

SC

Carolina jessamine

Who was Caroline, and why does she get two states named after her?

Believe it or not, there was no Caroline at all. "Carolina" is the Latin form of "Charles." Carolina (North and South were originally just one state) was named to honor England's Kings Charles I and Charles II and France's King Charles IX.

Carolina wren

Venus's-flytraps, wild plants that eat meat, grow only in North and South Carolina.

What are palmettos, and why is South Carolina so fond of them?

Palmettos are just what they sound like—baby palm trees with fan-shaped leaves. The trees helped South Carolina soldiers win one of the first battles of the Revolutionary War, which they fought from a fort built with soft palmetto logs. The British cannonballs sank right into the spongy wood!

SOUTH DAKOTA

SD

Pasqueflower

NICKNAME: THE COYOTE STATE
STATEHOOD: 1889
CAPITAL: PIERRE
STATE FLOWER: PASQUEFLOWER
STATE BIRD: CHINESE RING-NECKED PHEASANT

Thousands of years ago you would have found small three-toed horses, sabre-toothed tigers, and camels in the Badlands.

What's so bad about the Badlands?

The Badlands are a region in South Dakota of steep cliffs and strange, spooky rock formations, carved by thousands of years of exposure to wind and water, and extreme temperatures. The Sioux Indians called the area "land bad" because it was so hard to live on and travel across. But some people think the layers of pink, orange, gold, green, blue, silver, gray, and brown rocks are beautiful.

Over 13 feet high and 42 feet long, "Sue" might be the biggest, meanest, and oldest known inhabitant of South Dakota. This famous *Tyrannosaurus rex* skeleton has been around for about 60 million years.

The men of Mount Rushmore: Who doesn't belong?

George Washington

Thomas Jefferson

Gutzon Borglum

Teddy Roosevelt

Abraham Lincoln

All these men belong, but Gutzon Borglum's face is not on the mountain. He designed South Dakota's Mount Rushmore, one of the largest stone carvings in the world. Each of the sixty-foot-tall presidents' heads was carved using dynamite and jackhammers.

No wonder the project, started in 1927, took workers fourteen years to complete—even though they were *dynamite* sculptors!

Chinese ring-necked pheasant

TENNESSEE

NICKNAME: THE VOLUNTEER STATE
STATEHOOD: 1796
CAPITAL: NASHVILLE
STATE FLOWER: IRIS
STATE BIRD: MOCKINGBIRD

Iris

Mockingbird

TN

Is Tennessee called the Volunteer State because its residents do lots of community service?

Not really. Tennessee has been known as the Volunteer State since 1847, when the United States was fighting the Mexican War. The government asked Tennessee for three thousand volunteer soldiers, and thirty thousand joined.

Graceland, Elvis Presley's mansion in Memphis, is the second-most visited home in the nation. Only the White House, where the president lives, gets more visitors.

Yee-haw! What Tennessee city is the home of country music?

Nashville is known as "Music City, USA." A country music radio show called *The Grand Ole Opry* started in Nashville in the 1920s. It helped make country music popular. *The Opry* is the longest-running live radio show in the world.

What Tennessee frontiersman was famous for wearing a coonskin cap?

Frontier settler Davy Crockett won hundreds of shooting contests as a young man. He later served in the army in the early 1800s and was then elected to Congress three times. Crockett said, "I leave this rule for others when I'm dead: Be always sure you're right—then go ahead."

TEXAS

NICKNAME: THE LONE STAR STATE
STATEHOOD: 1845
CAPITAL: AUSTIN
STATE FLOWER: BLUEBONNET
STATE BIRD: MOCKINGBIRD

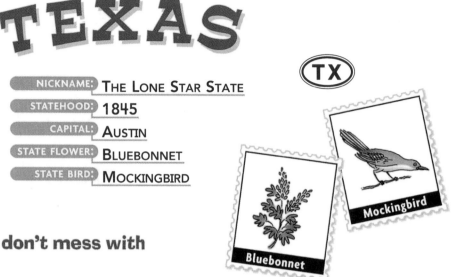

TX

Bluebonnet

Mockingbird

Why is it best if you don't mess with Texas?

Texas has always been fiercely independent—not the kind of state you want to mess with! In fact, Texas was once its own country, with its own flag, which had one star on it to symbolize Texas alone. (That's why it's called the Lone Star State.) During the Texas Revolution in the 1830s, when Texas won its independence from Mexico, 187 volunteers defended a fort known as the Alamo for thirteen days. All the Texans at the fort were killed, but Texas leader Sam Houston went on to win the revolution by inspiring his soldiers with the battle cry, "Remember the Alamo!"

True or false: A nodding donkey is an animal you'll find in a Texas zoo.

False—but you will find them in Texas oil fields. People drill for oil all over Texas with pumps called "nodding donkeys." The pumps are called this because that's what they look like as they pump up and down, bringing oil up to the surface.

Do all Texans wear cowboy boots and ten-gallon hats?

Not today, but many did more than a hundred years ago when cowboys rode horses to herd cattle north from Texas. They also wore:

- spurs, to make their horses go faster;
- chaps, to protect their legs from rain, thorns, and cattle horns;
- bandannas, to keep dust off their faces;
- Stetsons, the most popular kind of cowboy hat, to keep the sun off their heads.

Texas is so big that different parts of the state have completely different climates—it could be snowing in the north and blazing hot in the south on the same day!

Did you know that one out of every three cowboys was either African American or Mexican?

UTAH

Sego lily

Seagull

UT

NICKNAME: THE BEEHIVE STATE
STATEHOOD: 1896
CAPITAL: SALT LAKE CITY
STATE FLOWER: SEGO LILY
STATE BIRD: SEAGULL

Will you get lots of bee stings in the Beehive State?

No. Utah is nicknamed the Beehive State not for bees, but in honor of the Mormons, a religious group that was the state's first white settlers. The Mormons believe in working industriously and living together in close communities the same way bees do. On the very first day they arrived in 1847, they got to work plowing and making ditches for water so they could farm Utah's dry land.

Why is it so hard to drown in Utah's Great Salt Lake?

The water of the Great Salt Lake is so salty that it's almost impossible to sink in it. The water is four times as salty as ocean water, which makes it very good for floating.

- Utah is home to the biggest dinosaur footprints in the world, made by a hadrosaurid (duckbill) dinosaur.
- Utah is home to more kids under the age of ten than any other state as a percentage of the population.
- A golden spike was hammered into the ground in 1869 at Utah's Golden Spike National Historic Site, where railroads connecting the country's east and west sides first met.

VERMONT

NICKNAME:	THE GREEN MOUNTAIN STATE
STATEHOOD:	1791
CAPITAL:	MONTPELIER
STATE FLOWER:	RED CLOVER
STATE BIRD:	HERMIT THRUSH

VT

Red clover

Hermit thrush

The National Rotten Sneaker Championship is held in Montpelier. People enter old sneakers, and winners get a new pair of shoes and a can of Dr. Scholl's foot powder. Being a judge for that contest stinks!

The Green Mountain State is the perfect nickname for Vermont because:

a) The name "Vermont" comes from the French *vert mont*, which means "green mountain."

b) Vermont has lots of green forests and beautiful mountains.

c) It's the name of Ben & Jerry's pistachio ice cream.

They're all true. . . . Well, except the one about the ice cream. Both forests and mountains are important to the Green Mountain State. Tourists come to see Vermont's forests change colors in the fall and to go downhill skiing in the winter.

How many trees does it take to make one gallon of maple syrup?

Four trees' worth (forty gallons) of sugar maple sap must be boiled down to make just one gallon of maple syrup. Vermont makes more maple syrup than any other state.

VIRGINIA

NICKNAME:	THE OLD DOMINION
STATEHOOD:	1788
CAPITAL:	RICHMOND
STATE FLOWER:	FLOWERING DOGWOOD
STATE BIRD:	CARDINAL

(VA)

Cardinal

Flowering dogwood

Why is Virginia called both a mother and a father?

Virginia is the Mother of Presidents, because eight presidents were born there: George Washington, Thomas Jefferson, James Madison, James Monroe, William Henry Harrison, John Tyler, Zachary Taylor, and Woodrow Wilson. The state is the Father of States, because eight other states were made from the land that used to be part of Virginia: Illinois, Indiana, Kentucky, Michigan, Minnesota, Ohio, West Virginia, and Wisconsin.

Did Pocahontas really save John Smith's life?

Maybe. Captain John Smith was the leader of Jamestown, the first permanent English settlement in America, founded in 1607. According to Smith, when he was captured by the powerful Indian leader Powhatan, Powhatan's eleven-year-old daughter, Pocahontas, threw herself on Smith so he wouldn't be killed. No one knows if the story is actually true, but even if it was made up, it had a powerful effect on establishing peace between the Indians and the colonists.

Match the Founding Father below with one of his claims to fame:

1. He said, "Give me liberty, or give me death!" at the Virginia Convention in 1775.

2. He was ambassador to France and served the first french fries in America at his Virginia home.

3. Washington, D.C., was built near his birthplace in northern Virginia to honor him.

A. George Washington

B. Patrick Henry

C. Thomas Jefferson

Answers: I-B 2-C 3-A

WASHINGTON

NICKNAME:	THE CHINOOK STATE
STATEHOOD:	1889
CAPITAL:	OLYMPIA
STATE FLOWER:	RHODODENDRON
STATE BIRD:	WILLOW GOLDFINCH

WA

Willow goldfinch

Rhododendron

Now Entering WASHINGTON STATE

Why is half of Washington wet and the other half dry?

The Chinook State was named both for the Chinook Indian tribe that lived there and for a pair of winds that affect the state's weather. The winds push rain clouds from west to east. But halfway across the state, they're stopped by the Cascade Mountains. Because the wind and clouds can't get past the peaks to the east side, much more rain falls on the west side of the Cascades.

Washington is the only state named for a president.

What famous Washington landmark blew its top?

The explosion of Washington's Mount St. Helens in 1980 was the largest volcanic eruption people have recorded in America. Ash turned the sky black while mud and lava flattened trees and houses. Fifty-seven people were killed. Within two weeks, ash from the eruption had fallen around the world.

WEST VIRGINIA

NICKNAME: **THE MOUNTAIN STATE**
STATEHOOD: **1863**
CAPITAL: **CHARLESTON**
STATE FLOWER: **BIG RHODODENDRON**
STATE BIRD: **CARDINAL**

WV

Big rhododendron

Cardinal

If there is a West Virginia, are there also North, South, and East Virginias?

Nope, just a West Virginia. The state was born when Virginia left the Union during the Civil War. The people in the western part of the state wanted to stay with the Union, so West Virginians formed their own state.

How do you build an airport on top of a mountain?

You chop off its top! To build the Charleston airport, workers had to chop the tops off mountains and fill in the surrounding valleys with tons of dirt to make an area flat enough for airplanes.

John Henry vs. a machine. Who won?

West Virginia folktales tell of a railroad worker named John Henry. Henry was a real man, a super-strong African American who pounded spikes into railroad ties faster than anyone alive. Once he tried to pound faster than a mechanical drill—and he succeeded. But he died later that night.

What potential miner disaster is no minor disaster?

Coal mining has been the Mountain State's main industry for more than a hundred years. Being a miner is a dangerous job because mines can collapse and trap workers inside. Miners can also die from black lung disease from breathing in too much coal dust.

WISCONSIN

WI

NICKNAME: **THE BADGER STATE**
STATEHOOD: **1848**
CAPITAL: **MADISON**
STATE FLOWER: **WOOD VIOLET**
STATE BIRD: **ROBIN**

Wood violet

What are Holsteins, Jerseys, and Guernseys?

Old Wisconsin saying:
"The world is your cow,
but you'll have to do
the milking."

(Here's a hint: When they need to be milked, they moooooove very slowly.) They're different kinds of cattle. Wisconsin's two million cows make more milk than any other state. The state also produces lots of other dairy products like cheese and butter. No wonder people who live in America's Dairyland are proud to be called Cheese Heads.

Robin

Test your pioneer skills!

Laura Ingalls Wilder, author of the Little House books, was born in a log cabin near Pepin, Wisconsin, in 1867. She traveled by covered wagon all over the Midwest during her youth, and her books describe pioneer ways on the American frontier. Her first book, *Little House in the Big Woods*, is about growing up in the forest in Wisconsin. Can you match each object below with the item pioneers used to make it?

1. candy
2. doll
3. balloonlike ball

A. corncob
B. pig's bladder
C. snow and molasses

Answers: 1-C 2-A 3-B

WYOMING

NICKNAME: THE EQUALITY STATE

STATEHOOD: 1890

CAPITAL: CHEYENNE

STATE FLOWER: INDIAN PAINTBRUSH

STATE BIRD: MEADOWLARK

WY

Indian Paintbrush

Meadowlark

Also called the Cowboy State, Wyoming probably has more true working cowboys today than any other state. You might imagine that cowboys live on flat land where nothing changes for miles and miles. But *Wyoming* is a Delaware Indian word that means "alternating valleys and mountains." Wyoming has mountains in the west and plains in the east.

Thousands of pioneers traveling west on the Oregon Trail carved their names in a landmark called Independence Rock, near Casper.

What did Wyoming women get to do before any other American women?

They got to vote, all the way back in 1869! The rest of the country's women didn't get to vote until 1920. Wyoming also had the first woman to serve on a jury, the first female mayor, and the first female governor. No wonder it's called the Equality State.

I *faithfully* shoot ten thousand gallons of hot water more than one hundred feet in the air every eighty minutes, on average. Who am I?

Old Faithful, in Wyoming's Yellowstone National Park, is America's most famous geyser. A geyser is a special kind of hot spring that shoots water into the air. Yellowstone, the world's oldest, largest, and most popular national park, has more than two hundred geysers plus lots of other cool wonders like boiling mud.

WASHINGTON, D.C.

[OR DISTRICT OF COLUMBIA]

NICKNAME: **CAPITAL CITY**
ESTABLISHED: **1800**
FLOWER: **AMERICAN BEAUTY ROSE**
BIRD: **WOOD THRUSH**

(DC)

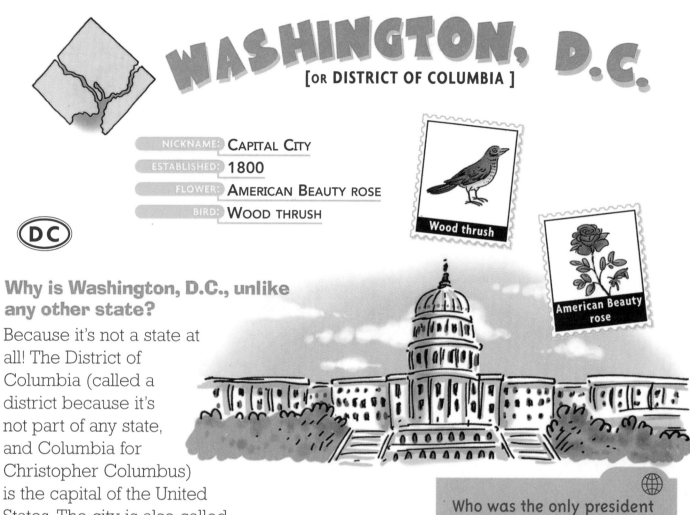

Wood thrush

American Beauty rose

Why is Washington, D.C., unlike any other state?

Because it's not a state at all! The District of Columbia (called a district because it's not part of any state, and Columbia for Christopher Columbus) is the capital of the United States. The city is also called Washington, D.C., after President George Washington, who chose the site in 1791 to be the nation's capital.

Who was the only president who didn't live in the White House?

George Washington, who died before it was finished.

Will there ever be a fifty-first state?

There might be, one day. Some people think Washington, D.C., should be the fifty-first state. Others think it should be Puerto Rico, an island territory about nine hundred miles southeast of Florida. We'll just have to wait and see. Who knows? One day the Stars and Stripes may even have fifty-*two* stars on it!

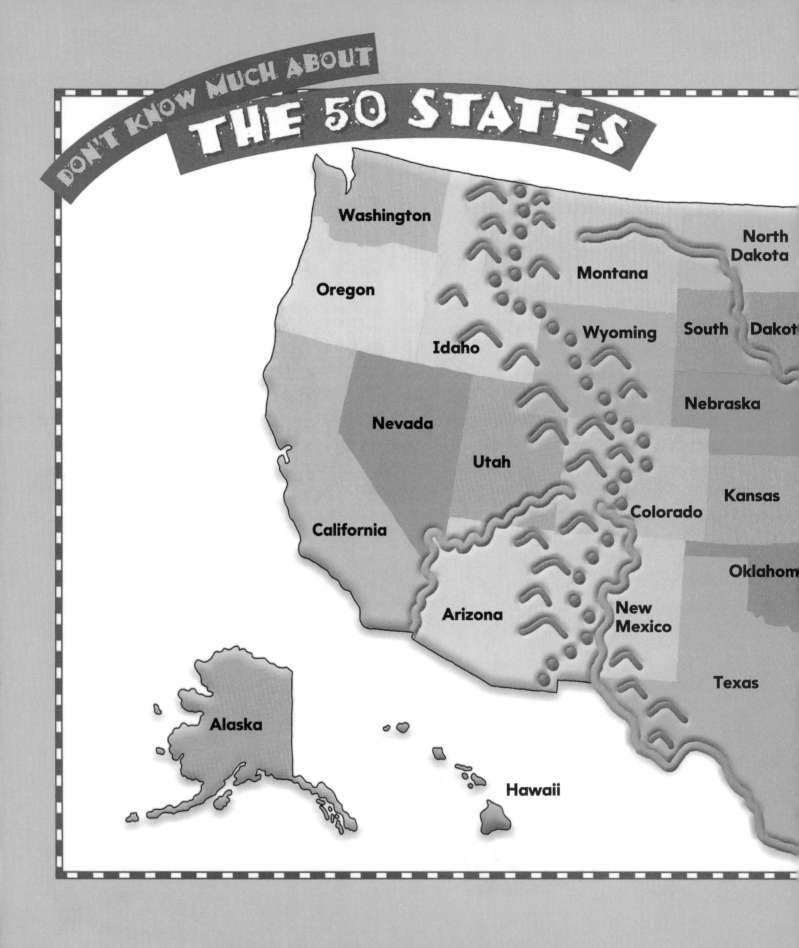

THE 50 STATES

Washington

Oregon

Idaho

Montana

North Dakota

Wyoming

South Dakota

Nevada

Utah

Nebraska

California

Colorado

Kansas

Arizona

New Mexico

Oklahoma

Alaska

Texas

Hawaii

THE UNITED STATES

Minnesota

Wisconsin

Michigan

Iowa

Ohio

Indiana

Illinois

Missouri

Arkansas

Kentucky

Tennessee

Vermont

Maine

New Hampshire

Massachusetts

New York

Rhode Island

Connecticut

Pennsylvania

New Jersey

Delaware

Maryland

West Virginia

Virginia

North Carolina

South Carolina

Alabama

Georgia

Florida

Mississippi

Louisiana

The Thirteen Original Colonies

Connecticut
Delaware
Georgia
Maryland
Massachusetts
New Hampshire
New Jersey
New York
North Carolina
Pennsylvania
Rhode Island
South Carolina
Virginia